SNAKE

SNAKE

Rebecca Stefoff

BENCHMARK BOOKS

MARSHALL CAVENDISH
NEW YORK

Benchmark Books
Marshall Cavendish Corporation
99 White Plains Road
Tarrytown, New York 10591-9001

Illustrations by Jean Cassels

Library of Congress Cataloging-in-Publication Data
Stefoff, Rebecca, date
Snake / Rebecca Stefoff.
p.   cm. — (Living things)
Includes bibliographical references and index.
Summary: Examines the physical characteristics and behavior of
snakes and describes six different kinds.
ISBN 0-7614-0412-0 (lib. bdg.)
1. Snakes—Juvenile literature. [1. Snakes.] I. Title.
II. Series: Stefoff, Rebecca Living things.
QL666.O6S797 1997   597.96—dc21   96-39106 CIP AC

Photo research by Ellen Barrett Dudley

Cover photo: *The National Audubon Society Collection/Photo Researchers, Inc.*,
John Mitchell

The photographs in this book are used by permission and through the courtesy of:
Peter Arnold, Inc.: Hans Pfletschinger, 2; Martin Wendler, 6; Andrew Odum, 10–11;
John Cancalosi, 11 (right), 12, 24 (left); J.F. & Nicolas Hellio/Van, 14; BIOS
(Compost/Visage, 16; Steve Kaufman, 17 (top); Michael Doolittle, 17 (bottom);
Norbert Wu, 19 (bottom); Matt Meadows, 20; Luiz Claudio Marigo, 23; John S.
MacGregor, 26. *The National Audubon Society Collection/Photo Researchers, Inc.*:
John Mitchell, 7, 22 (left); François Gohier, 8, 9; S.L. & J.T. Collins, 10 (left);
Ferraro/Jacana, 13; Chet Tussey, 15; Gregory Dimijian, 18, 25 (bottom); Karl H.
Switak, 19 (top), 21; Steinhart Aquarium, 22–23; E.R. Degginger, 25 (top);
Jim Grace, 32. *Animals Animals:* Joe McDonald, 24 (right)

Printed in the United States of America

3 5 6 4 2

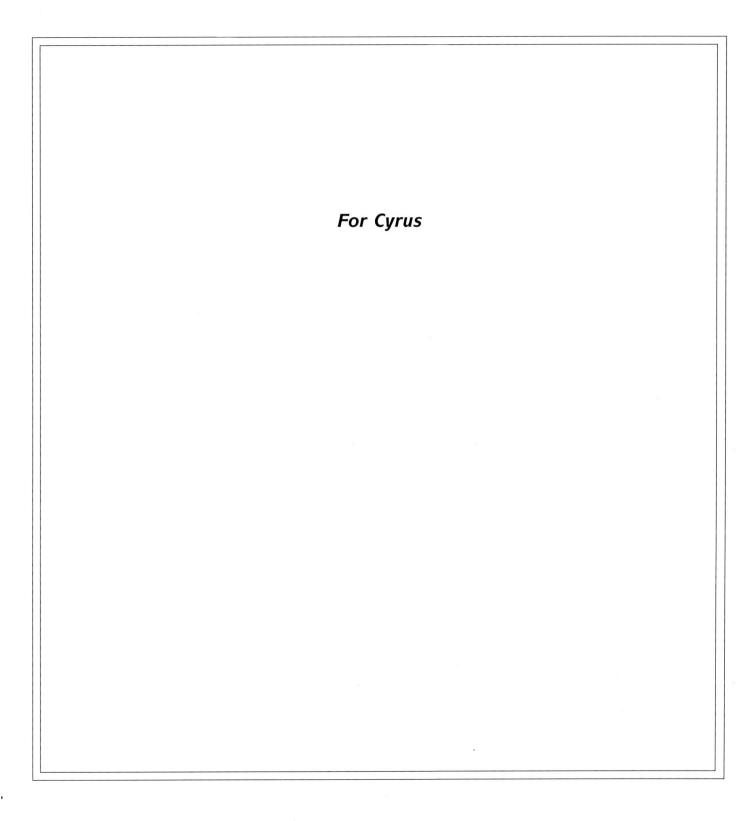

For Cyrus

yellow anaconda swimming, South Ameria

Pope's tree viper

What animal has no arms or legs but can swim and climb trees? Did you guess "snake"? You're right. Snakes are amazing animals.

7

red-sided garter snakes

Most snakes live alone. But some snakes get together in big, squirmy piles and spend the cold winter months sleeping together in dry caves or holes.

When spring comes, the snakes wake up and look around. Then each one slithers off on its own until winter.

red-sided garter snakes

scarlet king snake, Florida

California king snake

During warm weather you might find a snake
curled up on a leaf or a rock, dozing in the sun.

Snakes can't get warm from eating or from snug-
gling in a nest. They need the sun's heat to stay
warm. This is why no snakes live in the coldest parts
of the world, close to the North Pole and the South
Pole. But they live almost everywhere else.

10

western coral snake, Arizona

twin-spotted rattlesnake, Arizona

Snakes love hot places, like tropical rain forests and deserts. The hot parts of the world have more snakes than anywhere else. But snakes stay out of the sun during the hottest part of the day. Even a snake can get too hot.

These snakes are at home in the desert. Their long, skinny bodies can glide safely among the sharp spines of the cactus. And their skin is made of tough scales that protect them from the burning sand.

black-headed python

ringed snake

banded sea snake

All snakes can swim if they have to, but some snakes spend most of their lives in lakes and rivers. They glide silently along just under the surface of the water, looking for frogs or fish to eat. They stick their heads above the water when they need to breathe.

The striped snake on the coral reef is a sea snake. Sea snakes live in the warmest parts of the ocean, eating fish. Some of them never come out onto the land at all.

reticulated python

Can you find the snakes in these pictures? Lots of snakes that live in forests are colored to match tree bark and leaves.

The snakes blend into the trees until they are almost invisible. They are hidden from other animals that might want to eat them. And if a tasty bird or lizard comes by—zip! The snake darts out of hiding to snatch up a meal.

whip snake, Malaysia

In tropical forests, some snakes live high in the trees and never touch the ground. Tree snakes like the ones on this page are called "flying snakes." These snakes can't really fly, but they can spring through the air from tree to tree.

rhino viper

Not all snakes match the things around them. Many poisonous snakes stand out with bright colors, stripes, or spots. Perhaps these colors are the snake's way of saying, "Watch out! Stay away from me!"

See the yellow and red snakes curled on the tree branch? They are called green pythons. They will turn green when they are about two years old. Until then, the bright colors make the young pythons look like dangerous, poisonous snakes. This keeps the young pythons safe and gives them a chance to grow up.

18

eyelash viper, Costa Rica

long-nosed tree snake eating lizard, Southeast Asia

All snakes are hunters. They eat lizards, birds, fish, and even other snakes. Every year snakes help farmers around the world by eating millions of rats, mice, and insects that would nibble on the farmers' crops.

young green tree python eating wild mouse

The biggest snakes in the world are the anacondas, boas, and pythons. These snakes wrap themselves around the animals they catch and squeeze them to death.

Snakes don't take bites of their meals—they swallow them whole. The largest snakes can open their mouths far enough to swallow a whole pig or goat, an inch at a time. It takes a snake all day to swallow something as big as a pig.

Burmese python

anaconda

boa constrictor, Brazil

black-tailed rattlesnake   *hooded cobra*

Some snakes can be dangerous to people. All of the snakes on these pages are poisonous. The rattle-snake and the coral snake live in North America.

Snakes are afraid of people. When a snake hears you coming, it will slide away. Even a poisonous snake won't hurt a person unless it is surprised or scared. Snakes are much more interested in mice and frogs than they are in you.

yellow eyelash viper

northern pine snake

The next time you see a
snake, stop for a moment.
Treat the snake with respect
and don't get too close. But
take a good look. Remember
all the wonderful and useful
things snakes do.

27

A QUICK LOOK AT THE SNAKE

Snakes belong to a group of animals called reptiles. Lizards, turtles, alligators, and crocodiles are also reptiles. All reptiles have scaly skins and are cold-blooded, which means that they need heat from the sun to warm their bodies.

There are about twenty-seven hundred kinds of snakes in the world. Most snakes lay eggs, but a few kinds give birth to live young. Very large snakes have no natural enemies. Small and middle-sized snakes are eaten by eagles, hawks, roadrunners, racoons, wild dogs, wild cats, and wild hogs.

Here are six kinds of snakes along with their scientific names in Latin and a few key facts:

WESTERN DIAMONDBACK RATTLESNAKE

Crotalus atrox   (cro TAY lus AY trox)
Can grow up to seven feet long (2 meters). Lives throughout western United States, often in rocky areas. When disturbed, rattles hard, leathery rings at the end of tail to produce a buzzing sound. Bite is poisonous.

INDIGO SNAKE

Drymarchon corais   (dry MAR kon COH rayce)
Largest snake in North America. Grows to ten feet long (3 meters). Has very shiny dark blue scales. Lives in southeastern United States, especially Florida, and south to Brazil. Fast-moving, eats other snakes as well as mice and fish. Protected in United States as an endangered species.

COMMON GARTER SNAKE

Thamnophis sirtalis   (tham NO fis sear TAY lis)
Generally twenty to twenty-eight inches long (50–71 cm). Lives in northern United States and southern Canada. Dark color helps snake absorb sun's heat.

ANACONDA

Eunectes murinus
(YEW nek tees myew RYE nus)
World's heaviest and second-longest snake. Biggest known specimen weighed 330 pounds (150 kg) and was thirty feet long (9 meters). Lives in Amazon rain forest of South America. Swims well and climbs trees easily. Has a much smaller relative, the yellow anaconda.

HORNED VIPER

Cerastes cerastes   (seh RAS tees seh RAS tees)
Average length is twenty-eight to thirty-two inches (71–81 cm). Lives in desert areas of North Africa and the Middle East. Has two short, sharp horns, possibly to protect eyes from sand. All vipers are poisonous.

29

RETICULATED PYTHON

Python reticulatus
(PY thon reh tih kew LAY tus)
World's longest snake. Longest recorded python was thirty-two feet long (10 meters). Most measure twenty to thirty feet (6–9 meters). Slender grayish-brown body with black markings. Common throughout Southeast Asia and the Philippines.

Taking Care of the Snake

Today many kinds of snakes are in danger from people, who catch snakes to sell as pets or to make their skins into shoes and purses. People are also cutting down forests and changing other places where snakes live. We need to protect forests, deserts, swamps, and other wild places so that snakes and all the other creatures that share their world will always have a place to live.

Find Out More

Demuth, Patricia. *Snakes*. New York: Grosset & Dunlap, 1993.

Hess, Lilo. *That Snake in the Grass*. New York: Scribner's, 1987.

Maestro, Betsy. *Take a Look at Snakes*. New York: Scholastic, 1992.

Markle, Sandra. *Outside and Inside Snakes*. New York: Atheneum, 1995.

Parsons, Alexandra. *Amazing Snakes*. New York: Knopf, 1990.

Simon, Seymour. *Poisonous Snakes*. New York: Four Winds Press, 1981.

Index

Rebecca Stefoff has published many books for young readers. Science and environmental issues are among her favorite subjects. She lives in Oregon and enjoys observing the natural world while hiking, camping, and scuba diving.

speckled king snake